The Quick and Dirty Introduction to Cybersecurity

Lloyd Kaufman with GPT-3

The Quick and Dirty Introduction to Cybersecurity

Lloyd Kaufman with GPT-3

ISBN 978-1-7777210-6-0

Bootstrap IT

A division of DBC Technology Services Inc.

bootstrap-it.com

office@bootstrap-it.com

Contents

What Is Cybersecurity?

Cybersecurity is the practice of protecting your computer networks and user data from unauthorized access or theft. This can include using firewalls, antivirus software, and password protection, as well as educating users on how to stay safe online.

Cybersecurity problems can be classified into four categories: accidental problems, malicious problems, design flaws, and implementation flaws. Accidental problems are caused by user error, such as clicking on a phishing email. Malicious problems are caused by cybercriminals, such as ransomware or malware. Design flaws are inherent in the design of the software or hardware, while implementation flaws are introduced during the software or hardware's implementation.

In recent years, cybersecurity has become an increasingly important issue. Data breaches and hacking incidents are becoming more common, and can have serious consequences for businesses and individuals. The importance of cybersecurity cannot be overstated, and it is essential that everyone understands the basics of cybersecurity in order to protect themselves online.

There are many reasons why it is important to understand cybersecurity. Perhaps the most important reason is that cybercrime is on the rise. The FBI reported that total losses from ransomware alone jumped by more than 225% in the U.S. in 2020. In addition, the cost of cybercrime has been estimated at $945 billion per year globally. Cybercrime can take many forms, including ransomware attacks, data breaches, and phishing scams.

Data breaches cost organizations lagging in their security automation deployment an average of $6.03 million. These breaches can have serious consequences for businesses, including financial losses, loss of customers, and damage to reputation.

Individuals are also at risk from cyberattacks. In addition to the risk of financial losses, data breaches can also expose individuals to identity theft and other forms of fraud. It is therefore essential for individuals to take steps to protect their personal information online.

The main difference between cybersecurity problems for individual consumers and for large organizations is the scale of the problem. For consumers, the main worry is that their personal data will be stolen or compromised in some way. For large organizations, the worry is that their entire network will be hacked, leading to theft of confidential data or even destruction of critical systems.

One way to reduce your risk of being targeted by a cyberattack is to understand the basics of cybersecurity. By understanding how hackers operate and what kinds of attacks are common, you can take steps to protect yourself online.

The importance of cybersecurity cannot be overstated. Everyone should take steps to protect themselves online by understanding the basics of cybersecurity.

Cybersecurity threats and tools, protecting yourself and your business, responding to cybersecurity incidents, and managing backup and recovery are critical topics for any business. This book will provide you with a high-level introduction.

You will learn about the different types of cybersecurity threats that exist and how to protect your business from them. You will also learn about the different types of cybersecurity tools and how to use them effectively.

In addition, you will learn how to respond to a cybersecurity incident and manage backup and recovery. This book is an essential read for any business owner who wants to stay safe online or for aspiring IT professionals.

—-

Note that there are other titles in the Quick and Dirty Introduction series[1]. Feel free to check them out.

[1]https://www.amazon.com/dp/B09R4ZRLB6

Understanding Cybersecurity Threats

Cybersecurity threats come in all shapes and sizes, and can be difficult to understand and defend against. In order to best protect your devices or network from these threats, it is important to first understand what they are.

First of all, the criminals standing behind most of the worst threats are often known as hackers. A hacker is someone who uses his knowledge of computers and technology to break into networks and steal information or disrupt service. Hackers can use a variety of methods to gain access to networks, including exploiting security vulnerabilities or using social engineering techniques like phishing scams.

The following are some common IT security threat categories:

Malware is a broad term used to describe a variety of malicious software programs that are designed to harm or disable computers. Malware can include viruses, ransomware, spyware, Trojans and other types of harmful programs. These programs can be installed on computers through a variety of means, including email attachments, infected websites, and pirated software. Once installed, they can damage files, steal information or passwords, or even hijack the computer to use it in criminal activity.

Phishing is a technique used by cybercriminals to attempt to steal personal information such as usernames, passwords, and credit card details by pretending to be a trustworthy entity in an electronic communication. The most common way this is done is by sending an email that looks like it's from a legitimate organization such as a bank, credit card company, or online store. The email will usually ask the recipient to click on a link or open an attachment that will take them to a fake website where they are asked to enter their personal information. Phishing can also occur through text messages and social media platforms.

Spear-phishing is a type of targeted attack where an attacker sends a message to a *specific* individual or organization, hoping to trick the recipient into clicking on a malicious link or opening an infected attachment. The goal of spear-phishing is usually to steal sensitive data or gain access to systems and networks.

Spyware is a type of malware that can be installed on a computer without the user's knowledge, typically to track or record user behavior. It can also be used to steal personal information, such as passwords, or to display unwanted advertising.

Ransomware is a type of malware that encrypts files on a computer or mobile device, then demands a ransom payment to unlock them. The encryption may be so strong that it's impossible to decrypt the files without the right key or code.

Social engineering is the process of manipulating people into performing actions or divulging confidential information. It can be used to gain access to passwords, financial information, or other sensitive data. Social engineering attacks can be carried out through email, phone calls, or in person.

Denial of service (DoS) is a type of cyberattack that deliberately makes a machine or network unavailable to its users. By flooding the target with useless traffic, the attacker can prevent legitimate users from accessing it. This can be done by overwhelming the system with requests, overloading its resources, or crashing it completely.

Trojans are a type of malware that tricks users into installing it on their systems. Once installed, the trojan can perform a variety of malicious activities, such as stealing data or passwords, spying on the user, or even hijacking the system's resources to mine cryptocurrencies.

Rootkits are software programs that allow attackers to gain privileged access to systems without being detected. Once installed, rootkits can hide their presence from system administrators and security tools, allowing the attacker to maintain control of the system undetected. Rootkit installation can often be accomplished using standard user privileges, making them difficult to detect and remove.

Botnets A botnet is a collection of bots. Botnets can be used for malicious purposes such as launching DDoS attacks, stealing data, and distributing malware. (A *bot* is a software application that performs automated tasks over the internet. Typically, bots are used to automate routine tasks such as checking email, monitoring online auctions, or conducting web searches.)

Identity theft is the fraudulent use of another person's name, Social Security number, credit card number, or other personal information to obtain money or goods.

—-

As frightening as that list is, you're not getting the complete picture unless you can also visualize all the terrible things that can happen to your devices and data even without the help of criminals.

A natural disaster, such as a hurricane or tornado, can damage IT systems and infrastructure. A fire in a data center can destroy equipment and cause a power outage and data loss. Human error, such as entering the wrong command or deleting files by mistake, can also lead to IT disasters. Hardware failures, such as hard drive crashes or motherboard failures, can also result in lost data and disrupted operations.

In other words, you're always going to be at the very edge of complete disaster. Unless, of course, you plan ahead to both prevent trouble wherever possible, and to mitigate its impact when prevention doesn't work. That's going to be the subject of the rest of this book.

Understanding Cybersecurity Tools

One of the most important steps you can take to protect yourself from cybercrime is to learn about the different tools you can use as part of a cybersecurity effort. In this article, we will introduce some of the most common tools used in cybersecurity and explain why they are essential for defending your systems against attacks.

As a business owner, developer, or human being, you know that cybersecurity is important. You may have also heard that there are a variety of tools you can use as part of your defensive efforts. But what are these tools? And how do they work?

Here's a useful list. We'll introduce them one at a time through the rest of this chapter.

- Patch management
- Anti-virus software
- Privilege management
- Firewalls
- Intrusion detection/prevention systems
- Network monitoring tools
- User access control mechanisms
- Penetration testing tools
- Vulnerability scanning
- Log management

Only the first few of those tool categories are normally associated with consumers - the rest are best deployed and administrated by server professionals. But having a general understanding of how they all work has value for anyone.

Now let's dig a bit deeper.

Patch management

Patch management is the process of managing patches, or updates, for software and/or firmware. Patch management includes identifying available patches, retrieving the patches, testing the patches to ensure they will not harm systems or data, and deploying the patches in a controlled manner.

Patch management is used in cyber defense operations to keep systems secure by ensuring that all known vulnerabilities are patched. Patch management software can help automate the patch deployment process, making it easier and faster to deploy patches.

Anti-virus software

Antivirus software is one of the most basic tools used in cybersecurity. It is used to detect and remove viruses from your computer system. Antivirus software scans your computer for known viruses and removes them if they are found. It also monitors your system for any new or unknown viruses, which it will then quarantine or remove if necessary.

Antivirus software is essential for protecting your computer against malware infections, which can damage or destroy your data files or even allow someone to remotely control your computer. By using antivirus software regularly, you can help protect yourself from these types of attacks.

Privilege management

Privilege management is a technique used in security operations to limit the access of users and systems to resources based on their role or need-to-know. This allows organizations to reduce the risk of unauthorized access and data theft, while still providing authorized users with the necessary tools and information they need to do their jobs.

Privilege management solutions typically use role-based access controls (RBAC) to determine which users are granted access to which resources, and can also include features such as password complexity requirements, session timeouts, and audit logs.

RBAC controls determine who can access which resources in a network, based on their job role. RBAC assigns specific privileges to individual roles, rather than users, so that administrators can easily manage user permissions. When a user attempts to access a resource, the RBAC system checks the user's role against the permissions assigned to that role. If the user has permission to access the resource, they are allowed to proceed; if not, they are denied access.

RBAC is often used in conjunction with other security measures such as firewalls and authentication systems. It is an effective way of managing large networks with many users and complex security requirements. By assigning specific roles and permissions to different users, RBAC allows administrators to create tailored security systems that meet the needs of their organization.

##Firewalls

A firewall is a device or software that sits between your computer and the Internet and helps protect it from unauthorized access. It does this by allowing only authorized traffic through its filters while blocking all other traffic. This includes both incoming traffic (from the Internet) and outgoing traffic (to the Internet). Firewalls also provide other security features such as intrusion detection, which alerts you when someone attempts to hack into your system, and packet filtering, which allows you to control what type of traffic is allowed through the firewall.

Firewalls are an important part of any cyber defense strategy because they help protect both individual computers as well as networked environments such as businesses, schools, and universities. They work by preventing unauthorized access to systems using a variety of methods such as IP blocking, and port blocking.

Some popular hardware firewall solutions include the following:

- Cisco ASA
- Juniper SRX Series
- Palo Alto Networks PA Series

Linux software firewalls include:

- iptables
- Firewalld
- Shorewall
- IPCop

There are many consumer-grade firewall software solutions on the market today. Some of the more popular ones include:

- Windows Firewall
- MacOS X Firewall
- Sophos UTM

Intrusion detection systems

Intrusion detection systems (IDS) are software or hardware tools that monitor a computer system or network for signs of malicious activity. They can be used to detect intrusions, attacks, and other unauthorized activities.

IDS work by inspecting all traffic passing through the monitored system or network. They look for patterns that indicate malicious activity, such as unusual traffic flows, unexpected packets, and strange file modifications. When an IDS detects something suspicious, it alerts the system administrator so they can take action.

There are a variety of different types of IDSs available, including host-based IDSs (HIDS), network-based IDSs (NIDS), and hybrid IDSs. HIDS monitors individual hosts on a network for signs of intrusions. NIDS monitors all traffic passing through a specific network segment for signs of attack. Hybrid IDSs combine features from both HIDS and NIDS systems in order to provide more comprehensive protection.

Many enterprise hardware firewall systems include IDSs among their features. IBM's QRadar is an example of a commercial standalone tool. Open source IDS tools include Snort.

Intrusion prevention systems

An intrusion prevention system (IPS) is a computer security system that monitors a network or systems for malicious activity or policy violations. It is a type of security appliance that is placed in-line between two networks and monitors all traffic going in and out of the networks. IPSs are typically used to protect against attacks such as denial of service, SQL injection, cross-site scripting, and malware infections.

When an attack is detected, the IPS can take action such as blocking the traffic, shutting down the offending device, or sending an alert to the administrator. IPSs can also be used to enforce corporate security policies by restricting access to certain websites or applications.

Network monitoring tools

Network monitoring tools are used in defense operations to detect and prevent network attacks. Network attacks can include denial of service attacks, malware infections, and data breaches. Network monitoring tools allow security analysts to identify malicious activity on the network and take action to stop it.

Network monitoring tools work by scanning the network for devices and then mapping out the network. The tools will then identify any issues with the network and report it back to the user.

User access control mechanisms

User access control mechanisms work by verifying the identity of a user before granting that user access to a system or its resources. Common methods of verifying user identity include checking a user's username and password, scanning a user's fingerprints, or reading a user's retina.

Retinal scans for security work by scanning the patterns of blood vessels in the retina. This information is unique to each person and can be used for identification purposes. Retinal scans are considered very reliable and accurate forms of identification, and they are often used in security settings where high levels of authentication are required.

Penetration testing tools

Penetration testing is the process of using various tools and techniques to identify security vulnerabilities in systems or networks. These vulnerabilities can then be exploited to gain access to sensitive data or systems. Penetration testing tools allow testers to simulate real-world attacks on systems, in order to find and fix security flaws before they can be exploited by hackers.

Note that we've written a separate book on penetration testing: The Quick and Dirty Introduction to Penetration testing[2].

Vulnerability scanning

A vulnerability scanner is a type of security software that is used to identify potential security vulnerabilities on a computer or network. These scanners can be used to scan for common vulnerabilities such as open ports, missing patches, and weak passwords. They can also be used to scan for more specific vulnerabilities such as those that are found in specific applications or operating systems.

There are a variety of vulnerability scanning tools available, including Nessus, OpenVAS, and Qualys. These tools allow organizations to scan their networks for vulnerabilities and to determine the severity of those vulnerabilities. Vulnerability scanning can help organizations identify and address security flaws before they can be exploited by attackers.

Log management

Log management is the process of managing and analyzing log files to help identify and troubleshoot issues with a system or application. Log files are typically generated by servers, applications, or devices and can contain information about user activity, system performance, errors, and other data. The goal of log management is to collect, monitor, and analyze this data to help identify issues and improve the overall health of the system or application.

Some popular log management tools are Splunk, ELK Stack, Graylog, and Logstash.

---

[2]https://www.amazon.com/dp/B09R3Y72KH

Protecting Yourself

As technology advances, so do the methods that cybercriminals use to exploit users and steal data. Fortunately, there are many steps you can take to protect yourself and your personal devices from these threats.

One of the most important things you can do is keep your devices and software up-to-date. Many cyberattacks take advantage of vulnerabilities that have been fixed in newer versions of software, but haven't been updated by users yet. Be sure to install all available updates for your devices and applications as soon as they become available.

You should also use strong passwords. A strong password should be at least eight characters long, include a mix of letters, numbers, and symbols, and not be something easily guessed like your name or birthday. You should also never use the same password for multiple accounts.

Another important step is to install a good antivirus program on all of your devices. Effective antivirus programs scan files and email attachments for malware infections and help protect against other online threats such as phishing scams. There are many different antivirus programs available, so be sure to choose one that best suits your needs.

You should also be careful when clicking on links or opening attachments in emails, especially if they come from unfamiliar sources. Cybercriminals often use phishing scams to try and get users to click on malicious links or download infected attachments. If you aren't sure whether a link is safe or not, it's best not to click on it until you can verify its legitimacy with someone else.

Many home WiFi networks are vulnerable to attack. This is because many people do not take the necessary precautions to secure their networks. There are a few things you can do to help protect your home WiFi network from security breaches:

1. Use a strong password
2. Update your firmware regularly
3. Make sure your WiFi network is encrypted and use (at least) the WPA2 protocol
4. Keep the software - especially the web browsers - on all your devices up-to-date

There are a number of ways to protect your personal privacy online. One of the simplest is to use a pseudonym or alias when signing up for websites and services. This will help keep your real name and contact information private. You can also use privacy-friendly search engines like DuckDuckGo that do not track or store user data.

You can increase your privacy by using a Virtual Private Network (VPN). A VPN encrypts all of your traffic and hides your IP address, making it difficult for others to track you online.

It is also important to be careful with the information you share on social media. Make sure you are only sharing information with people you trust, and be aware of the settings on each platform so that you can control who sees what.

Additionally, you can install ad blockers and tracking blockers to prevent websites from tracking your web browsing habits or use purpose-built secure browsers like Brave[3]. Finally, you can use encryption tools to protect the data that you share online.

---

[3]https://brave.com/

Protecting Your Business

As a business owner, you likely understand that cyberthreats are a real and growing concern. From ransomware to data breaches, there are many ways for hackers to target your company's digital assets. However, there are also steps you can take to protect your business from these threats.

Creating a security plan

Any business should have a comprehensive security plan. An effective security plan is one that covers all the bases, from data protection to physical security. It should be tailored to the specific needs of the business, and it should be updated regularly as new threats emerge.

The first step in creating a security plan is to assess your risk level. What are you most worried about? Hackers? Viruses? Theft? Once you know what your biggest risks are, you can start taking steps to mitigate them.

Data protection is key in any security plan. You need to make sure that your confidential information is safe from prying eyes, whether it's stored on computers or on paper files. You should also have a backup plan in case of a data breach.

Be particularly careful about *where* you store your data. Make sure that any confidential information is kept in a secure location and access is limited to authorized users only. And if you ever suspect that your system has been compromised, be sure to report it immediately so that appropriate action can be taken.

Physical security is another important element of any security plan. You need to make sure that your premises are protected against intruders, both inside and outside the building. Security cameras and alarm systems can help deter thieves and vandals, while locks and gates can keep unauthorized people out of the property altogether.

Employee training is also essential for creating a secure environment. Employees need to be aware of how to protect themselves online and how to identify potential threats before they become a problem. They should also be aware of company policies for using strong passwords, encrypting data wherever possible, and dealing with data breaches or other emergencies.

Another important step is to stay up-to-date on the latest security threats. Hackers are constantly evolving their tactics, so it's important that you keep track of the latest threats and vulnerabilities. You can do this by subscribing to security newsletters or attending industry conferences.

Enforcing security policies

Every company should have a comprehensive security policy that addresses the following:

- Personnel security (background checks, training, etc.)
- Information security (access controls, passwords, encryption, etc.)
- System and network security (firewalls, intrusion detection/prevention systems, etc.)

By following these tips, you can help protect your business from cyberthreats and keep your data safe from harm:

1. Require that even private devices connected to the company networks are properly patched and secured.
2. Educate employees on safe online practices, such as not opening suspicious emails or clicking on links in them.
3. Restrict access to sensitive data to only those who need it and creating strong passwords for all accounts.
4. Regularly back up important data so it can be restored in the event of a cyberattack.

Responding to Incidents

A plan for responding to cybersecurity incidents is important because it can help an organization to quickly and effectively respond when something does happen. The plan can also help to minimize the damage that is caused by the incident and can help to ensure that the organization's systems are secure afterwards.

Initial incident response

When a cybersecurity incident occurs, the first step is to determine the extent of the damage and what systems have been compromised. Once this has been established, it is necessary to take steps to contain the damage and prevent it from spreading. This may include disconnecting infected systems from the network, removing malware, and restoring data from backups.

Believe it or not, the best way to disconnect infected systems from the network after a security incident is to physically unplug the system from the network. Another way is to disable the system's network connection by disabling the network adapter or turning off the system's wireless capability.

Alternatively - if those solutions aren't possible - you may want to consider at least temporarily tightening up your firewall settings.

Determining the cause

Once the incident has been contained, it is necessary to investigate how it happened and identify the perpetrators. You will usually also need to work with law enforcement agencies and/or hire a cybersecurity firm to conduct an investigation.

The process of identifying the causes of a security incident is typically a multi-step process that includes gathering information about the incident, analyzing that information, and then developing hypotheses about the causes of the incident. Once hypotheses have been developed, further investigation is typically conducted to determine which hypotheses are most likely to be accurate.

Gathering information

This can be done by conducting an investigation and interviewing employees who may have knowledge of the incident. Once the source of the breach has been identified, investigators can gather evidence from computers and other electronic devices that may have been used in connection with the attack. They can also review security footage to try to identify any suspects.

Analyzing information

The first step in security breach analysis is to identify the cause of the breach. This can be done through forensic investigation, which includes reviewing network activity logs and system files to find out what happened and when. Once the cause is identified, steps can be taken to prevent similar breaches from happening in the future.

Next, it's important to determine which systems or data were affected by the breach. This can be done by identifying which systems were accessed during the attack and analyzing what was accessed or stolen. Once this information is known, it can be used to develop a response plan that focuses on protecting those systems and data from future attacks.

Finally, it's important to communicate with affected employees or customers about the breach. This includes informing them of what happened, what information was compromised, and what steps they need to take to protect themselves from identity theft or other types of fraud.

Preventing repeat incidents

Finally, steps must be taken to prevent future incidents from occurring. This may include implementing new security measures, training employees on how to identify and respond to threats, and conducting regular risk assessments.

We've already (briefly) discussed risk assessments in the "Understanding Cybersecurity Tools" chapter. There, you were introduced to tools for penetration testing and vulnerability scanning. Such tools can be used as part of formal security audits - which can often be required for legal and regulatory protocols.

Security audits work by assessing the security of an organization's IT infrastructure and identifying any potential vulnerabilities that could be exploited. The auditor will then recommend steps that can be taken to mitigate these vulnerabilities. Security audits are typically performed by a third-party assessor, such as a security consultant, who will review the organization's systems and processes and compile a report detailing any findings.

One example of industry compliance is the Payment Card Industry Data Security Standard (PCI-DSS), which is a set of requirements designed to ensure that all companies that process, store or transmit credit card information maintain a secure environment.

To comply with PCI-DSS, organizations must implement strong security controls and processes based on the 12 requirements of the PCI Data Security Standard. These requirements cover topics such as securing cardholder data, protecting against malware and hacking, and maintaining a vulnerability management program.

The 12 requirements of the PCI DSS are:

1. Install and maintain a firewall configuration to protect cardholder data
2. Do not use vendor-supplied defaults for system passwords and other security parameters
3. Protect stored cardholder data
4. Encrypt transmission of cardholder data across open, public networks
5. Use and regularly update anti-virus software
6. Develop and maintain secure systems and applications
7. restrict access to cardholder data by business need-to-know
8. track and monitor all access to network resources and cardholder data
9. Control access to cardholder data
10. Maintain a policy that tracks and monitors resource and data access
11. Test system security regularly
12. Assign responsibility and controls over information security

Regardless of whether your organizations is required to become PCI-DSS compliant, those 12 steps are valuable in and of themselves.

Backup and Recovery

There's a lot that can go badly wrong with your data. Some common causes of permanent data loss include:

- Deleted data: Accidental or intentional deletion of data can render it unusable
- Corrupted data: If data is not stored correctly or becomes damaged, it may be impossible to read or use
- Illegal access: Unauthorized access to confidential data can lead to privacy breaches, identity theft, and other security risks.

How would you or your organization be impacted by the sudden loss of key data? Would it mean facing significant financial hardship or inconvenience? Could your business pick up the pieces afterwards and continue to function?

Creating a data backup plan

When it comes to data backup plans, there are a few key things to remember. First and foremost, your plan should be tailored to your specific needs. What kind of data do you need to back up? What are the potential risks if that data were lost or corrupted? How much time and effort can you realistically devote to backing up your data?

Once you've answered those questions, there are a few basic steps that all data backup plans should include:

1. Back Up Your Data Regularly: This may seem like common sense, but it's important to actually follow through with

regular backups. Ideally, you should back up your data at least once a week (or more often if necessary).

2. Store Your Backups in Multiple Locations: Ideally, you should have multiple backups of your data stored in different locations (e.g., on different hard drives or external drives, on different computers/servers, etc.). That way, if one location is damaged or lost, you still have access to your data elsewhere.
3. Use an Appropriate Backup Method: There are many different ways to back up your data - from simple manual copying of files onto an external drive, to using online backup services - so choose the method that best suits your needs and comfort level.
4. Test Your Backup Plan Regularly: It's important not only to create a good backup plan but also to test it regularly so that you know it will actually work when needed!

Creating a data recovery plan

A data recovery plan is a document that outlines how you will recover your data in the event of a disaster. It should include detailed instructions on how to backup your data, how to restore your data, and who is responsible for each step of the process.

The key ingredients of a data recovery plan are:

1. A backup strategy - You need to have a way to back up your data regularly so that you can restore it if it is lost or damaged.
2. A disaster recovery plan - You need to have a plan for recovering your data in the event of a disaster. This should include detailed instructions on how to restore your data and who is responsible for each step of the process.
3. A testing strategy - You need to test your backup and disaster recovery plans regularly so that you know they will work when you need them.

Building the right plan requires that you fully understand how your organization uses its data. These three metrics are important tools for figuring that out:

- The Recovery Point Objective (RPO) is a measure of the acceptable amount of data loss in the event of a disaster. The RPO specifies how much data can be lost and the organization can still meet its business objectives.
- The Recovery Time Objective (RTO) is a measure of how long it should take an organization to recover from a disaster. The RTO specifies how long it can be before services are restored to users.
- The Maximum Tolerable Outage (MTO) is the maximum length of time that an organization can tolerate without its critical services.

Next Steps: Launching a Cybersecurity Career

What's next for you?

Cybersecurity professionals are in high demand, with an estimated shortfall of 1.5 million workers globally. Cybersecurity careers offer a variety of opportunities to work in exciting and challenging environments, making it an appealing choice for those looking for a career change or those who want to enter the workforce for the first time.

This book has at least given you a bit of an overview into the cybersecurity industry as a whole. It's also shown you some of the key tools in play. Are you interested in diving deeper? Pick a technology (like Linux security administration[4]) or a field (like penetration testing[5]) and start learning!

Whatever your next steps, I hope you experience success and satisfaction.

Good luck!

Lloyd Kaufman and GPT-3

Check out some of our other titles in the Quick and Dirty Introduction series[6]/.

And consider writing a review of this book. Sharing your experience with others can help the everyone in the community find exactly what they're after.

---

[4]https://www.amazon.com/gp/product/B08L74M8MN
[5]https://www.amazon.com/dp/B09R3Y72KH
[6]https://www.amazon.com/dp/B09R4ZRLB6

Made in United States
North Haven, CT
04 November 2026

21772024R00020